How to Smile

and really mean it

by C. Mahoney

Wad up a few pieces of paper.

Make a pile.

When someone walks by, hit them with one.

Toss another.

And another.

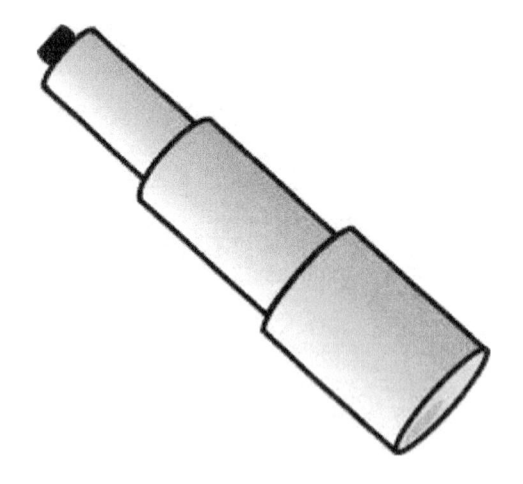

Grab an old toilet-paper roll.
Pretend that it is a telescope.
Say "Would you look at that" and hand it to someone.

Roar like a lion, loudly.
Then meow like a kitten.
Do this when you're with family or friends.
Don't explain.
If they express curiosity or surprise,
ask, "Do you have something against cats?"

Fill your mouth full of water.
Act like you are a whale.

Do this while someone is with you.

Eat a bowl of ice-cream, without a spoon.

Go to the library on a Saturday.
Walk down an aisle in the Fiction section.
Grab a book from any shelf that is eye-level.
Find a chair.
Read for an hour.
Return the book to the shelf.

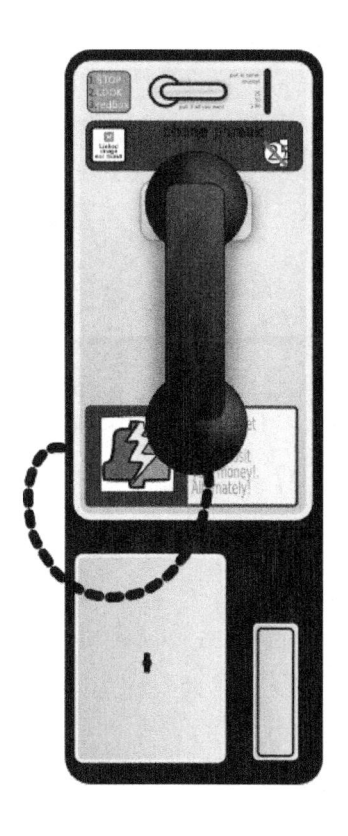

Find a payphone and make a call from it (to a friend).

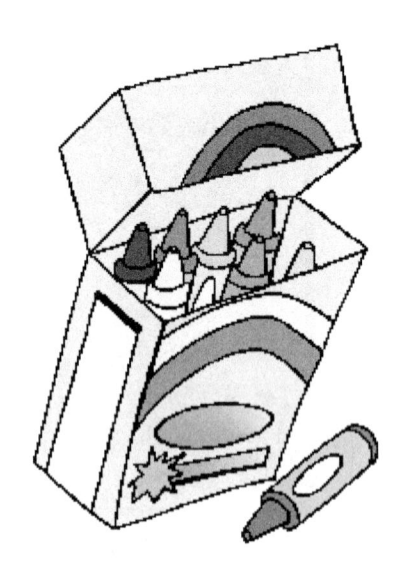

Buy a cheap box of sixteen crayons and use all of them in one picture.
Red.
Blue.
Green.
Brown.
Orange.
Black.
White.
Fill in every corner of the page.

Note: only clouds can be white.

You can draw stick people if you want.

Put on two different colored shoes and go out shopping,
in a mall or at Wal-Mart,
anywhere that people will more interested in looking for stuff to buy
than in checking you out.
Be bold.
Don't be afraid.
What is the worst that could happen?

Wear a tie all day for no reason.
Adjust it as you talk to someone,
your coworker, an employee at McDonalds, the stranger in the elevator.
How do you feel?
More important?
More serious?
Dressed up?
Hey, you are a big kid now.
You can wear what you want.
If someone asks you why you are wearing a tie,
reply with "Didn't you get the memo?"

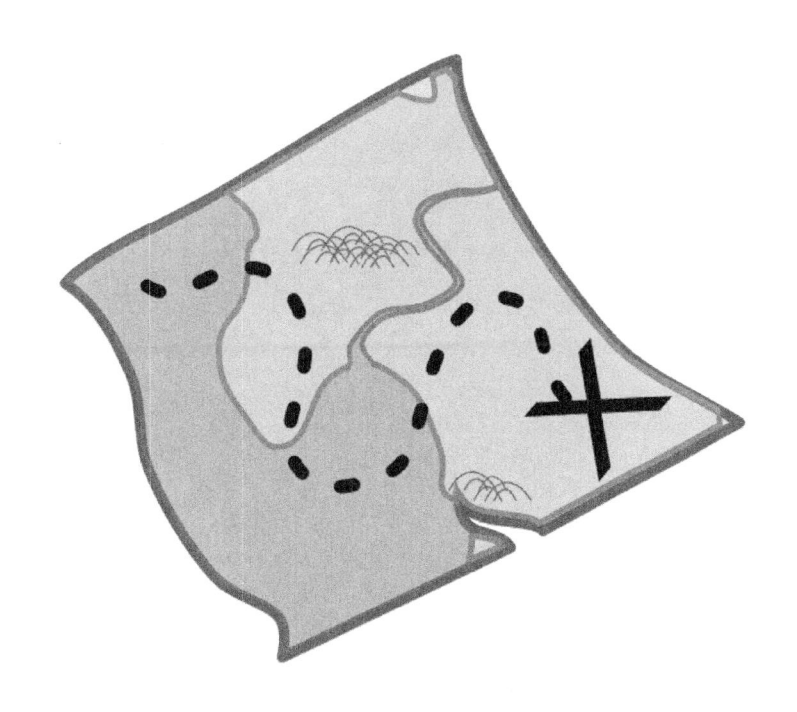

Hide something.
Make a treasure map.
Give it to someone and walk away.

Drink an entire glass of water without stopping to take a breath.

Have you NEVER done this before?

Oh, come on.

Try it.

Be sure to take a deep breath first.

Open a dictionary.

Pick a random word.

Text that word to a friend.

When they reply,

continue a conversation with that word as the catalyst.

Don't tell them what you just did.

Act natural.

Grab a piece of paper and a pen.

Draw a spiral in the center of the paper

and don't stop until you get to one of the four edges.

Then put it on your refrigerator at home

with a big A+ on it (in red).

GRAB A PEN.
DESIGN A MAZE.
HAND IT TO SOMEONE TO SOLVE.

TELL THEM YOU HAVE A CANDY BAR WAITING FOR THEM IF THEY CAN SOLVE IT IN FIVE MINUTES.

START COUNTING AS YOU WALK AWAY.

Touch someone.
Say "You're it."
Run away.

Look back over your shoulder from a distance.

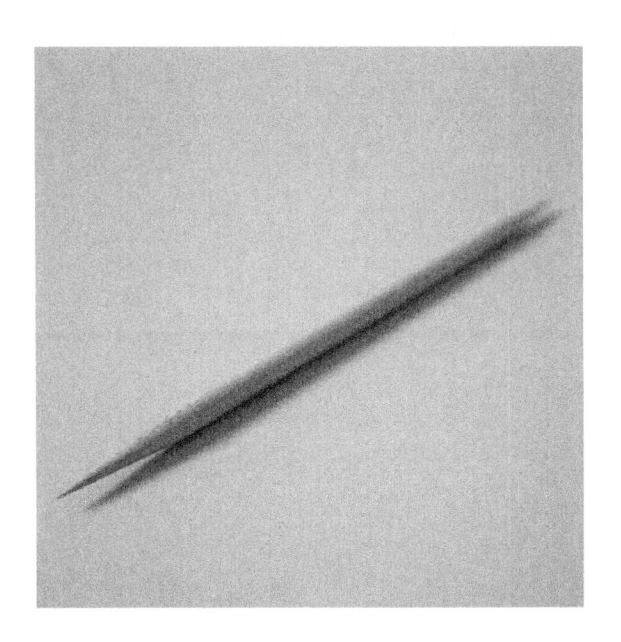

Fill a bowl with Cheerios.

Eat it with a toothpick.

Don't poke yourself in the eye.

Make a PBJ.

Eat it.

Have a tall glass of your favorite PBJ-friendly beverage on hand.

Drink hot chocolate.

Note: tiny little marshmallows are soooooo delicious.

Walk from one spot in your home to another with your eyes closed.

Slowly.

WATCH A TELEVISION SHOW WITH THE SOUND MUTED.

Watch a series of commercials with your eyes closed and see if you can determine what they are selling.

Shout it when you figure it out.

Open a box of saltine crackers.
Stack them as high as you can (like Jenga).

Use your non-dominant hand.

Hug someone you love.

Call a friend.

Speak in one-word sentences.

Let them fill the silent voids.

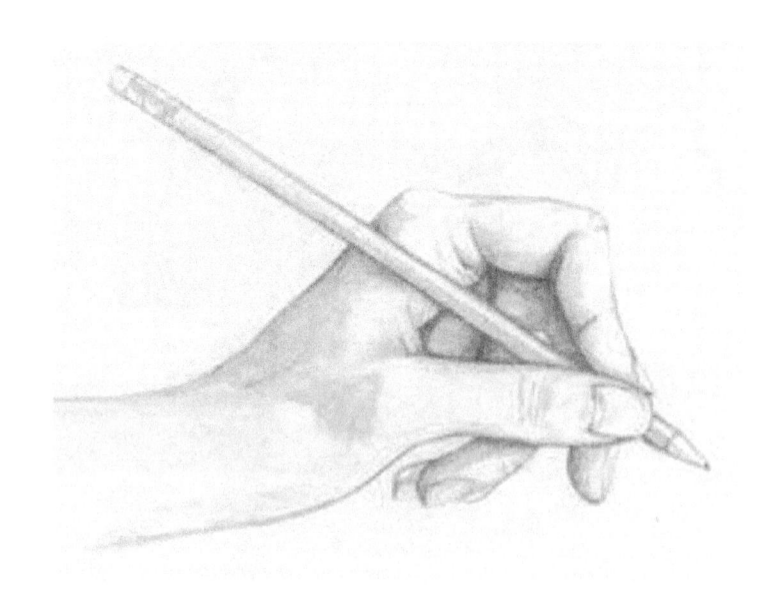

Grab a pencil and paper.

Find a hand-held mirror.

Draw yourself with your left hand.

Take a dog for a walk.
If you don't have one,
then visit a friend who does
and borrow their dog.

Talk to the dog the entire walk.

Make a paper airplane.

Go outside.

Throw it.

Again.

Again.

Wad up a piece of paper.
Grab a pot from the kitchen.
Make a sky-hook,
and jump-shot,
and a free-throw.

When you score say, "In your face."

Grab three eggs.
Practice juggling in the kitchen over the linoleum.

Stop when you are down to one egg.

Capture a bug with your hands.

Roly-polies are harmless.
Brown June bugs are harmless.
Green Japanese beetles are harmless.
Stay away from the bees.

Set a clock in your home an hour later.
Don't tell anyone.

If someone notices it and fixes it,
then change it again when they're gone.

Have a staring contest with someone.
Don't tell them what you are doing.
Just stare, without blinking.
When they blink or turn away, yell "I won" and do the victor's dance.

Go house shopping, for fun.

Drive around and look.

Don't stop. Don't get out. Just drive, slowly.

Talk about the great features that you see,

the yard, the fence, the trees, the second story...

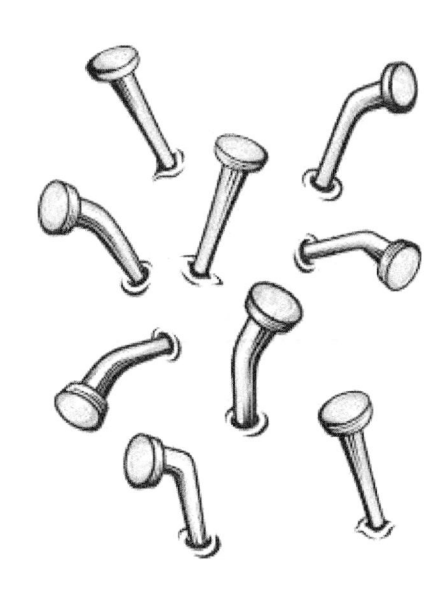

Grab a piece of wood, a hammer, and some nails.
Hammer all of the nails into the board, but be sure to bend every nail.

Take them out.
Try to straighten the nails.

Answer the phone with
"I won! I won! Woohoo!"

Play your air-guitar in front of your kids.
Make all the sounds.

When you finish, say "Thank you, very much" (like Elvis) and bow.

Put on your headphones or ear-buds.

Crank up the volume.

Dance.

When you're walking with someone,

challenge them to a race.

Say, "Ready, set, go" and then begin your slow-motion race.

Move in slow-motion and talk in slow-motion

as they pull away from you in regular motion.

Make your own invisible fireworks.
Make all the sounds and wave your arms.
Add the "Oohs" and "Ahhs".
Really get into it.

Set out your pots.
Grab a spatula.
Play the drums like you're a rockstar.

At night would be the best time for this activity.

Jump into a pool fully-clothed.

Have an imaginary argument with yourself, in public.

No cursing.

No insulting.

Just argue with intensity about something the other person said.

When your kid asks you something, say "Why?"
Keep repeating this word until they leave.
Try not to smile.
Try.

Walk like a dinosaur.
Wave your head.
Wave your hiney.
Stomp your feet.

Walk like a penguin.
Hands to the side.
Body rigid.

Walk like a robot.

Walk up to a lamp in your living room.

Rub it.

Make a wish aloud.

Walk away saying "I hope, I hope, I hope..."

Sit in a chair in the living room.

When someone comes in, get up and then down.

Crawl like a baby into another room.

Occasionally let out a childish "Wahhh."

Pet a cat.

**MAKE YOUR OWN SEE-SAW.
TRY IT OUT.**

Dance an Irish jig.

Don't speak a word for an hour.

Don't explain.

Don't write a note.

Just be silent.

Make up a new nursery rhyme, spontaneously,
about the next bug you see.

Note: even fake words can rhyme (Dr. Seuss-style).

Lie on your bed or couch.

Wave your arms and legs and say "I'm flying. I'm flying."

Lean over to the left and to the right, waving your arms.

Go to a large store.

Pretend that you are a doorman.

Stand there and open the door for people as they enter the store.

Be polite.

Walk outside.

Get down on your hands and knees.

Look for a four-leaf clover.

Get down on your hands and knees and act like a dog.
Do the things that dogs do.
Scratch.
Bark.
Beg.
Play.

Climb a tree.

Have a picnic in your front yard,

or the back,

or your neighbor's.

Go fishing.

"Moo!"

That's right, make the sound that a cow makes when people walk by.

Keep mooing and mooing.

Act like a flamingo.
Stand on one foot.

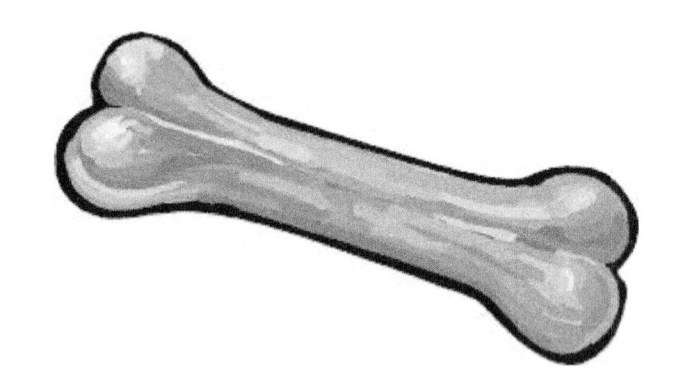

Bury a bone, without any tools.

Ask someone to scratch your back
as if you have an itch that just won't stop,
one you can't reach.
Keep them scratching and scratching,
lower, higher, lower, to the left, up, right...

Walk up to a complete stranger.
Give them a box labeled "Fragile."
Have them sign for it on a clipboard.
If they look confused, show them the line on the paper where it says
"Stranger."

Note: be sure to have already placed a candy bar and a nice note wishing
them a pleasant day inside the sealed box.

Watch cartoons.

Play with a ball.

Wear pajamas all day.

Rent your favorite series.
Stay up all night watching it.
Eat lots of popcorn.

Go out to eat with your family.
Make foldable nametags for everyone.
Pretend that you all just met for the first time.

Carry a rock and ruler all day.
Tell everyone you meet, "I rock. You rule."

Stand in front of a mirror
and pretend that you are blasting off in a rocket.
Make the sounds.
Shake and tremble.
Make the weird facial contortions.
Say, "Houston, I think we have a problem.
I forgot to buckle up."
Then float around the room, bumping into stuff.

Pretend you are a vampire.
Lie down on the couch.
Cover yourself with a blanket.
Tell the others in the room,
"I must sleep vile zee sun eez out. Eet ezz bad for me skin."
And laugh that villainous vampiry laugh as you disappear from view.

Wave to the people in the cars next to you at stoplights.

Set up two boxes in your yard.
Grab a stick and a ball and see how many smacks it takes you to get the ball to the box.

For best results, use an oddly shaped stick,
like a hammer or a wooden spoon.

Grab a broom.
Ride it like it is a pony.
Say "Getty-up" and make the sounds of a pony.

Sit in a chair.
Make the sounds of a racecar.
Turn to the right with wheels skidding.
Turn to the left with wheels skidding.
Up-shift on the straight-aways.

Walk up to a friend with your hands behind your back.
If they ask you how you are doing,
then pull your hands out from behind you and answer.
Note: Have already placed a colorful and clean sock on your hand.
It's now a sock puppet.
Make it talk.
Give it a funny voice.

Make a star badge and wear it all day.
When people ask about it, say "Oh, it's nothing.
My mommy gave it to me this morning for being a good kid."

Carry a piggy bank around with you all day.
If people ask, tell them it's your purse.

Be sure to have a few coins inside and give it a little shake to prove your point.

Stick out your tongue to everyone you meet today.

When someone asks you a question, hold your breath.
Hold it!
Hold it!
Let it out, apologize, and ask them to repeat the question.

Then, repeat what you just did…

*Stand on the curb
and pretend that you are riding a skateboard.*

Do a few tricks.

Yell "Surprise!" for no reason.

Write a number on a piece of paper.
Pin it onto your chest.
Get in an elevator.
When the door opens, sprint out the door…

Jump.
That's it.
Just jump, an inch, two inches, then as high as you can.
And say, "Ribbit."

Pretend that you are eating a burger.

Chew.

Close your eyes.

Say, "This is the BEST burger I ever ate."

Do this in front of friends when sitting at a table or desk.

Dance like a ballerina.

Note: this tactic is especially useful if you are male.

Play your invisible violin.

Make no sound.

Play with gusto.

Pretend that you are vacuuming the carpet.

Scrub extra hard on that one spot, over there.

Whistle while you work.

When at a restaurant, raise your hand and say "Ooh, ooh, pick me" when the waitress comes to your table.

Then when she gets to you say, "I forgot."

Put a sheet over your head,
and walk through your house making a low moaning sound.

Note: this is best done at night when others are drowsily making their way to the land of slumber.

Grab something that is NOT a jump rope, and jump, awkwardly.

Give a flower to a complete stranger,
and walk away.

Make fish-lips as you stand in line,

at the bank, at Taco Bell, wherever.

Suck in those cheeks.

Pucker those lips.

Sing a song, any song.
This is especially successful when there is someone else in the room who does not expect it.

Give someone directions, without words.
Use your hands.

Pretend that you are a bird when someone asks you a question.

Tweet your response to them.

Pretend that you are a cheerleader during a conversation.

Eat a donut.
No, eat two.

Open a kid's drink.
Put the straw in it.
Squeeze it as hard as you can.

Play a game of Tic-Tac-Toe, with yourself.
Try to win.
Don't cheat.

Write yourself a letter.
Say lots of nice things.
Give yourself compliments.

Mail it.

Toss a Frisbee.
Go get it.
Toss it again.

Make a box that says "Lost and Found."
Put some cool stuff inside of it.
Leave it by the door and see what happens.

Get on your kid's bike.
Ride as fast as you can.
Feel the wind.

Grab a baseball cap and a fork.
Wave the fork over the hat.
Say "Abracadabra" and pull out something from the hat.

Note: be sure to place something in there first.

Sit in your car.
Pretend to drive.
"Zoom, zoom. Honk."

Pretend that you are a train.
"Choo-choo.
Chugga-chugga, choo-choo."
Move your arms like the wheels.

Sit in your front yard.

Watch the cars go by.

Wave.

Tonight,
once the sun has gone down and you've had enough to eat,
walk around the block,
just once,
and while you are walking
look at the plants that your neighbors have planted.

On a Sunday afternoon, get into your car and drive for two minutes.
One, two, three...one hundred twenty.
Wherever you are, pull over and get out.
Lock your car.
Walk home and look for the things near your home to your left and right that you NEVER see as you drive.
Enjoy!

(Don't forget to return to your car and get it).

Go to a fast-food restaurant,
any one will do.
Order a free cup of water.
Sit down at a table, sip your water, and listen to the sounds,
the conversations of other customers,
the banter between the workers,
the honks and engine revving outside.

Make a pitcher of Kool-Aid.
Grab a chair and little table and set up a Kool-Aid stand on the sidewalk outside of our home.
No signs.
Just you and your smile.
Offer a free cup to anyone who happens to walk by,
the old guy with his dog,
a kid on a bike...

smile

Printed in Great Britain
by Amazon